ANIMALS
—OF THE—
TUNDRA

Written by Richard Vaughan

Celebration Press
An Imprint of Pearson Learning

Tundra is the cold, barren land in the far north of the world. Sometimes it is called the frozen prairie because the winter temperatures are so cold it is hard for trees and plants to grow. Except for five to seven weeks in summer, the ground of the tundra is always frozen.

Animals and birds that live in the tundra have developed some special ways to survive in this cold and rugged land.

POLAR BEAR

Polar bears have a white fur coat and a thick layer of fat below their skin to keep them warm. The white fur helps the bears blend in with their snowy surroundings. Some of the polar bears' hair is hollow, allowing the warmth of the sun to go right through to their skin. Fur also covers the bottoms of the polar bears' feet to help them walk on the slippery ice and snow.

When polar bears are born, they are the size of a puppy, but they grow to be twelve feet long and weigh up to fifteen hundred pounds! Even though polar bears are very big, they are strong swimmers. Their favorite foods are fish and seals.

🌲 LEMMING 🌲

Lemmings are furry little mouselike animals that live in underground tunnels called burrows. Because the ground of the tundra is frozen, lemmings line their burrows with grass and moss to keep out the cold.

A lemming's fur is gray-brown, with a lighter color fur on the belly. Some lemmings' fur turns white during winter to help them hide against the snow while searching for food.

Lemmings raise large families with eight to ten babies. They eat grass, roots, plants, and insects. Lemmings have to be very careful outside their burrows because they are hunted by foxes, wolves, and owls.

SNOWY OWL

The snowy owl gets its name from its covering of white feathers. Being all white makes this owl very hard to see.

The snowy owl hunts by spreading its wings out wide and gliding slowly over the tundra. When it sees a fish or lemming, the owl swoops down and grabs it with its strong, sharp talons (clawed feet) and carries it away.

The snowy owl makes its nest on the cold ground of the tundra. It uses its body to form a warm, feathery blanket over the top of the chicks.

Snowy owls can grow to be two feet high. Their feathers stay white all year around.

MUSK OX

Musk ox are sometimes called Arctic buffalo. They are strong, short-legged animals that travel the tundra in herds.

A musk ox has two coats to keep it warm. The outer coat of hair is black and very long. It hangs down to the animal's feet and sways as it walks. Under this outer coat is a soft, wool inner coat that keeps its body warm.

Musk ox eat only plants, and must keep moving to find enough food. If the herd senses danger, the adults form a circle around the young.

Musk ox can grow to be eight feet long and weigh nine hundred pounds.

SNOWSHOE RABBIT

The snowshoe rabbit gets its name from its big, wide feet. The size and shape of these feet help it to hop on top of deep snow and to swim in the lakes.

Its white winter fur helps the rabbit hide on the snow. In summer the rabbit's fur changes to a reddish-brown color to match the bare earth and moss in its summer surroundings.

At birth snowshoe rabbits are less than three inches long, but they grow quickly and start hopping when they are three days old. They eat grass, tree bark, and plants.

CARIBOU

Caribou live in small herds of eight to twenty animals that roam the tundra in search of food. Their wide hooves with sharp edges allow the caribou to cross frozen surfaces and dig through the snow for food.

Caribou have a gray or light-brown summer coat that turns white in winter. Both male and female caribou grow long, sharp antlers to defend themselves. They eat grass, moss, shrubs, and tree bark, and can weigh more than 650 pounds.

GRAY WOLF

Gray wolves are the largest animals in the wolf family. These fierce hunters have excellent hearing, eyesight, and sense of smell. They also have strong claws, powerful jaws, and razor-sharp teeth.

Gray wolves live in packs of up to 30 animals. They hunt by outrunning their prey. A single wolf can bring down a deer, and a pack of wolves can run down a bull moose or large caribou.

The young wolves are called pups, and are raised by the entire wolf family until they are old enough to hunt.
Gray wolves
are known for their
loud howl.

WALRUS

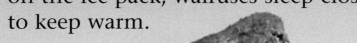

Walruses are often found in water, where it can be warmer than on the ice. Their skin has a thick layer of blubber to keep them warm in the cold Arctic sea. When they are on the ice pack, walruses sleep close together to keep warm.

A walrus has two sets of flippers that work like paddles in the water. It also has a bristly mustache and two long tusks on each side of its mouth. The tusks are used for digging up food from the bottom of the ocean. A walrus dives down to the ocean floor and stands on its head to dig up shellfish.

Weighing over a ton, walruses look slow and clumsy on land. But in the water they are fast and graceful swimmers. They can inflate pouches in their neck to keep them floating on the surface of the water while they sleep.

♨ WEASEL ♨

Weasels have long, slender bodies with short legs and a pointed head. In summer they have reddish-brown fur, which helps them blend in with the tundra's bare earth and moss. In winter the fur turns pure white to help them hide in the snow. An all-white weasel is also called an ermine.

Weasels hunt day and night for lemmings, rabbits, mice, and birds. They are excellent hunters because they can move with lightning speed. Their long, narrow bodies allow them to fit down burrows to find mice or rabbits. If a weasel catches more food than it can eat, it stores the extra food in its burrow for the long, cold winter.

Once a year, female weasels have a litter of four to six babies.

ARCTIC TERN

Arctic terns are white and gray, with long, pointed wings and tail. They have a black head with a narrow red beak and red feet.

Their slender features make them very fast and strong flyers. They streak along the surface of the ocean and quickly scoop up small fish and plankton for dinner. They also snap up flying insects right out of the air.

Arctic terns nest on the tundra through the short Arctic summer. By autumn the new chicks are strong enough to fly south with their parents.

The terns fly together in small flocks all the way to the South Pole. The long journey takes up to seven months. They return to the northern tundra again in spring.